WHO EATS WHAT?
SAVANNA
FOOD CHAINS

by Rebecca Pettiford

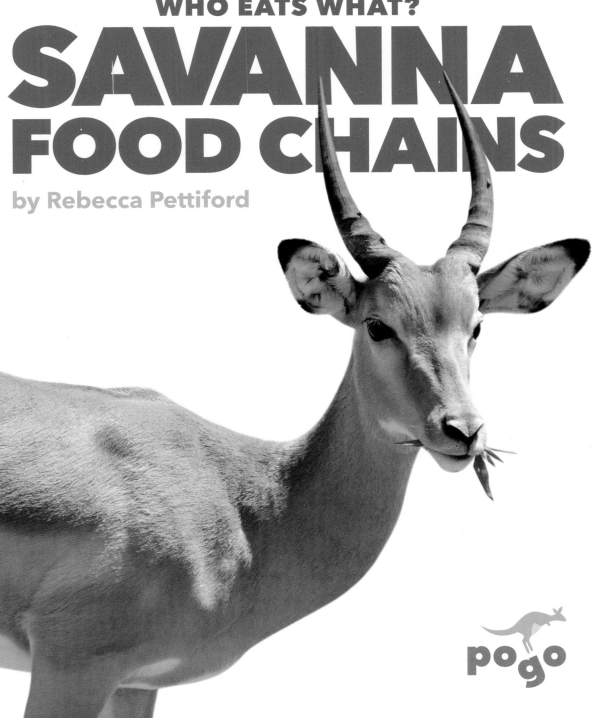

pogo

Ideas for Parents and Teachers

Pogo Books let children practice reading informational text while introducing them to nonfiction features such as headings, labels, sidebars, maps, and diagrams, as well as a table of contents, glossary, and index.

Carefully leveled text with a strong photo match offers early fluent readers the support they need to succeed.

Before Reading

- "Walk" through the book and point out the various nonfiction features. Ask the student what purpose each feature serves.

- Look at the glossary together. Read and discuss the words.

Read the Book

- Have the child read the book independently.

- Invite him or her to list questions that arise from reading.

After Reading

- Discuss the child's questions. Talk about how he or she might find answers to those questions.

- Prompt the child to think more. Ask: What other savanna animals and plants do you know about? What food chains do you think they are a part of?

Pogo Books are published by Jump!
5357 Penn Avenue South
Minneapolis, MN 55419
www.jumplibrary.com

Library of Congress Cataloging-in-Publication Data

Names: Pettiford, Rebecca, author.
Pettiford, Rebecca. Who eats what?
Title: Savanna food chains / by Rebecca Pettiford.
Description: Minneapolis, MN : Jump!, Inc. [2017]
Series: Who eats what? | "Pogo Books are published by Jump!." | Audience: Ages 7-10.
Identifiers: LCCN 2016028285 (print)
LCCN 2016029215 (ebook)
ISBN 9781620315729 (hardcover: alk. paper)
ISBN 9781620316177 (pbk.)
ISBN 9781624965203 (ebook)
Subjects: LCSH: Savanna ecology—Juvenile literature.
Food chains (Ecology)—Juvenile literature.
Classification: LCC QH541.5.P7 P484 2017 (print)
LCC QH541.5.P7 (ebook) | DDC 577.4/8—dc23
LC record available at https://lccn.loc.gov/2016028285

Editor: Jenny Fretland VanVoorst
Book Designer: Michelle Sonnek
Photo Researchers: Michelle Sonnek & Leah Sanders

Photo Credits: All photos by Shutterstock except: AdobeStock, 20-21b; Alamy, 3, 9, 12-13, 16-17, 20-21tm; Getty, 1, 14-15, 23; iStock, 8; Minden, 6-7; SuperStock, 5, 10-11, 19.

Printed in the United States of America at Corporate Graphics in North Mankato, Minnesota.

TABLE OF CONTENTS

CHAPTER 1

RAIN AND FIRE

In Africa, the **tropical** grassland **biome** is called the **savanna**. It is warm all year.

The wet season is May through October. The savanna gets about 20 inches (50 centimeters) of rain each month.

The dry season is November through April. It does not rain a lot. In the dry season, fires are common. Fires burn old grasses. Now new grasses can grow. Trees on the savanna have thick bark. It protects them from fire. Many animals on the savanna are fast. They can outrun fires.

WHERE ARE THEY?

The largest savanna is in Africa. Other savannas are in South America, India, and Australia.

= Savanna

CHAPTER 2
THE SAVANNA FOOD CHAIN

Savanna plants and animals need energy to live and grow. Food is energy. Plants make their own food. Animals eat plants and other animals.

A **food chain** shows how energy moves from plants to animals. Each living link in the chain eats the one before it.

baobab tree
(producer)

Grasses and trees are **producers**. They gather energy from the sun, soil, and water. Then they make their own food. They are the first link in the savanna food chain.

DID YOU KNOW?

Animals will eat different things to live. This means they are part of more than one food chain. When food chains cross, they make a food web.

Animals such as **gazelles** and zebras **graze** on grasses and leaves. So do elephants and rhinos. They are **consumers**, the next link in the chain. These animals gather in herds. This helps protect them from **predators**.

gazelle
(consumer)

lion
(predator)

Who are the predators? Animals such as lions and cheetahs. They hunt and eat consumers. They are the next link in the food chain.

Large predators will also eat smaller predators. For example, a lion will eat a baboon. A baboon eats mostly plants, but it will eat small animals, too.

DID YOU KNOW?

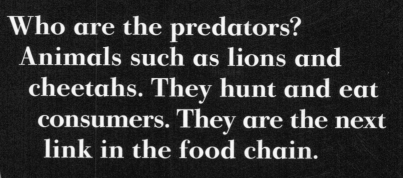

Hyenas are predators. But they are also a kind of animal called a **scavenger**. They eat already dead animal and plant material.

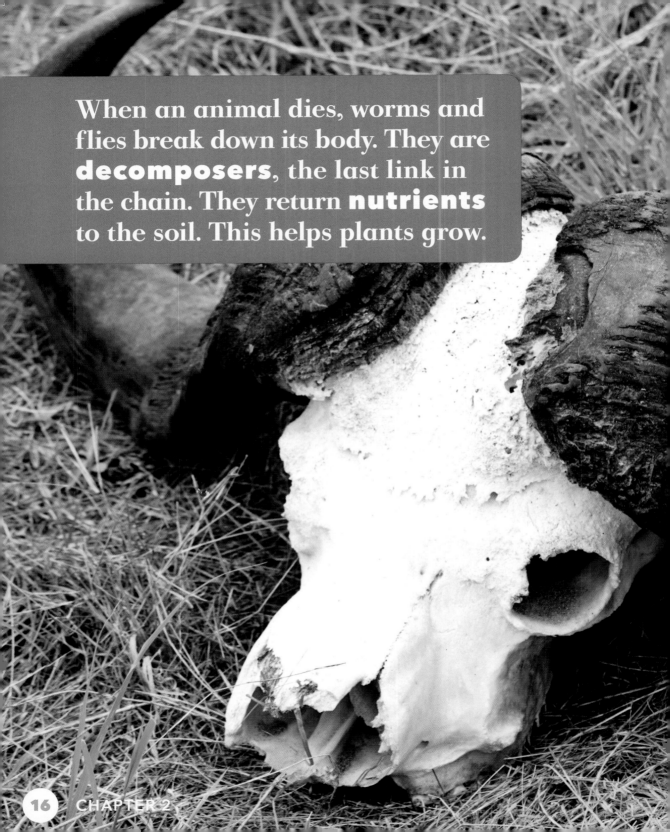

When an animal dies, worms and flies break down its body. They are **decomposers**, the last link in the chain. They return **nutrients** to the soil. This helps plants grow.

TAKE A LOOK!

One savanna food chain might look something like this:

Producer:
Grass

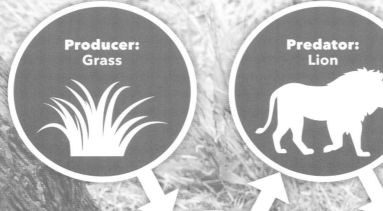

Predator:
Lion

Consumer:
Gazelle

Decomposer:
Worm

CHAPTER 3

FOOD CHAIN CLOSE-UPS

Let's look at a simple food chain. Grass grows on the savanna. A zebra eats the grass.

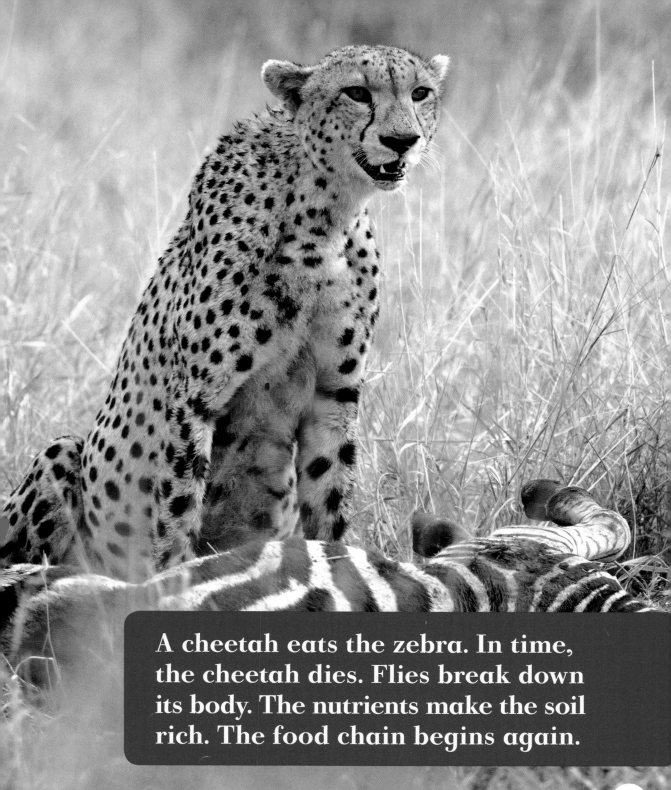

A cheetah eats the zebra. In time, the cheetah dies. Flies break down its body. The nutrients make the soil rich. The food chain begins again.

Let's look at another food chain.

1) This one starts with an acacia tree.

2) A giraffe eats its leaves.

3) A lion eats the giraffe.

4) The lion dies. Worms break down its body. Its nutrients help new trees grow.

The food chain continues!

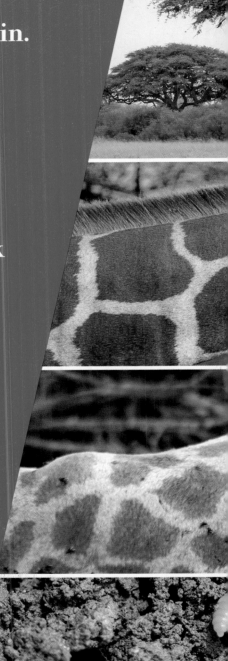

DID YOU KNOW?

When lions hunt, they work together. It is too hard for one lion to hunt a herd of animals.

ACTIVITIES & TOOLS

PLAY SAVANNA TAG

Play savanna tag with your friends! Your "savanna" can be a basketball court, a yard, or a driveway. You will want six or more players.

① Two players are lions.
   Four or more players are zebras.

② Lions stand in the middle of the savanna.
   Zebras stand at one end of the savanna.

③ Zebras must run from one end of the savanna to the other. Lions try to tag (eat) as many zebras as they can.

④ If a lion "eats" a zebra, the zebra must freeze. Zebras that reach the other side are free!

⑤ A tagged zebra becomes a lion in the next game. (On a real savanna, lions often grow in number when they have plenty to eat.)

⑥ If a lion starves (does not tag anyone), he or she must be a zebra next time. (On a real savanna, there are more zebras when there are fewer predators.)

GLOSSARY

biome: A large area on Earth defined by its weather, land, and the type of plants and animals that live there.

consumers: Animals that eat plants.

decomposers: Life forms that break down dead matter.

food chain: An ordering of plants and animals in which each uses or eats the one before it for energy.

gazelles: Small deer-like animals that have curved horns and yellowish-brown fur.

graze: Eating small amounts of plants throughout the day.

hyenas: Large, strong animals that eat flesh and are active at night.

nutrients: Substances that are essential for living things to survive and grow.

predators: Animals that hunt and eat other animals.

producers: Plants that make their own food from the sun.

savanna: A tropical grassland biome in Africa, South America, India, and Australia.

scavenger: An animal that eats already dead animal and plant material present in its habitat.

tropical: An area of the world with hot, wet weather.

INDEX

TO LEARN MORE

Learning more is as easy as 1, 2, 3.

1) Go to www.factsurfer.com

2) Enter "savannafoodchains" into the search box.

3) Click the "Surf" button to see a list of websites.

With factsurfer, finding more information is just a click away.